SAMADHI

Essence of the Divine

MIRABAI DEVI

SAMADHI
Essence of the Divine

MIRABAI DEVI

MIRABAI DEVI
FOUNDATION

Mirabai Devi Foundation, USA

Samadhi Copyright © Mirabai Devi Foundation, 2010

ISBN: 0-615-38131-6
EAN-13: 978-0-615-38131-2

Contributors:

Layout: John Rheaume and Kara Gilligan
Cover Art: Rey Tagle and Kara Gilligan
Photos of Mirabai: Dayna Resgio, Kate Bissinger
Back Cover Photograph: Mikki Willis
Drawing: Prema Spozdzial and Matt Hicks
Light Body Paintings: Prema Spozdzial

Prints of the Light Body Paintings by Prema Spozdzial cannot be made or used without the permission of the artist.

To Contact the artist, please go to **www.yogaprema.com** *or email* **prema@yogaprema.com**.

Contents

Dedications

I'd like to thank all those who helped to make this book possible.

John Rheaume for editing, graphic design and layout. Rey Tagle for cover art. Kara Gilligan for cover art, graphic design and layout.

Diane Baxter and Bridget Fonger for transcribing the original text. Bhavani for her copy editing. Mara Bright for additional editing. Jonni Wrestler for her support in seeing this book through to publication.

Prema Spozdzial for her paintings of light beings.

I'd like to acknowledge and thank the Avatars, both embodied and in spirit, who have illuminated my path.

I'd also like to thank the Self-realized teachers who have helped to inspire me and my worldwide spiritual family in South Africa, U.S. and worldwide. Without them, none of this would have been possible.

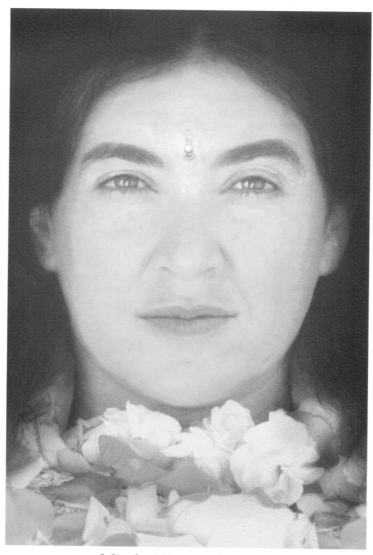

Mirabai Devi in Samadhi

All you have to do is let go.

Everything has always

been there for you.

The universe is taking care of you.

You are love.

You are everything.

Drop the false self,

and trust the process of life.

"Every moment you have a choice.
Are you going to choose ego or are you going to
choose Divine consciousness."

Mirabai Devi

Invitation to Divine Union

Union with the truth is the highest level of experience available to anyone with an open and devoted heart to God and to the Light. This divine state of deep God absorption is called Samadhi.

As you open up and contemplate the pages of this book, I invite you to take a journey deep into your own innermost being and experience the truth of these words for yourself. There can never be any substitute for direct experience.

Every word, meditation and message in this book has been written as a transmission of my own experience and designed to take you into your soul and remind you of the divine ever blissful state that is your eternal essence. The entire universe is within you. Everything you need for lasting happiness is already contained in every glowing cell of your body and soul. You lack nothing. The entire universe shines within you. Not a single star, not even a single grain of sand has been left out.

People talk about enlightenment but what does it really mean? It's so simple. There's no need to complicate it. Enlightenment is nothing more than the purest form of love. Not the conditional love that this world offers but the universal, passionate, ecstatic love that knows no bounds, no limits. It's a fierce uncompromising love that transcends all creeds and all religions. It transforms and frees from ignorance and darkness everything its light touches. Enlightenment involves being connected to the Light all the time.

When we come to experience the divine we realize that we

are made in this love, that our purpose and ultimate identity is love and always has been. Every step we ever took across the burning desert of suffering was to lead us back to this sacred, healing oasis of peace within our own hearts.

I invite you to drink deep from the well of your own divine being. You have waited long enough to taste the elixir of life. Why not let your thirst be quenched and don't forget for a moment that Samadhi is not only your birthright, it's your final and true destiny.

Since 1992, I have been experiencing Samadhi (Unity Consciousness) states. Anything can trigger these states, and they last for varied lengths of time.

My longest experience of Samadhi was for six weeks in 1992. Since then, I have experienced Samadhi states on a regular basis.

Almost anything can trigger a Samadhi state, the chirping of birds in a tree, or a walk in nature. But the most common causes are deep meditation, and darshan with a Master.

During darshan, the Teacher activates an awakening of your soul. They say that it takes only "one look, one touch" of one who is "there" to awaken you. It happens in a split second. In the old days, the ancients would go up the mountains to fast and pray, or chant, or dance and sing, depriving themselves of sleep for many nights, in order to gain even a glimpse of the underlying unity of all life- to realize their own, true nature.

They say that it takes much tapasya (austerities) to reach enlightenment. Tapasya is the burning away of karma, or dross, through purifying devotional practices and actions. For example, karma yoga, which means action devoted to God.

13

For some, many arduous hours are spent in hundreds of in-depth yogic practices. I am sure that in previous lifetimes all of this was played out for me. In this life, I was blessed with what I now know to be an activation of the memory of Samadhi states that I had attained in previous yogic lifetimes.

In 1992, my first meetings with spiritual teachers triggered these "memories" of Samadhi. Since then, they have spontaneously occurred.

These states, although very blissful and ecstatic, took a hard toll on my body. While reading Paramahamsa Yogananda's book, *Autobiography of a Yogi*, I recognized what was happening to me as "Savikalpa Samadhi." Paramahamsa Yogananda describes it as follows: "In the initial states of God-communion (Savikalpa Samadhi) the devotee's consciousness merges in the Cosmic Spirit; his life force is withdrawn from the body, which appears 'dead' or motionless and rigid. The yogi is fully aware of his bodily condition of suspended animation. As he progresses to higher spiritual states (Nirvikalpa Samadhi) however, he communes with God without bodily fixation and in his ordinary waking consciousness, even in the midst of exacting worldly duties."

Yogananda further explains, "The distinguishing qualifications of a master are not physical, but spiritual. Numerous bewildered seekers in the West erroneously think that an eloquent speaker or writer on metaphysics must be a master. Proof that one is a master, however, is supplied only by the ability to enter, at will, the breathless state (Savikalpa Samadhi), and by the attainment of immutable bliss (Nirvikalpa Samadhi).

The Rishis have pointed out that solely by these achievements may a human being demonstrate that he has mastered maya, the dualistic cosmic delusion. He alone may say, from the depths of realization, "Ekam Sat" (only One exists).

"When there is duality because of ignorance, one sees all things as distinct from the Self," Shankara, the great monist, has written. "When everything is known as the Self, not even an atom is seen as other than the Self... As soon as knowledge of the Reality has sprung up, there can be no fruits of past actions to be experienced, owing to the unreality of the body, just as there can be no dream after the waking."

When the first Samadhi experiences started I had almost no awareness of the body. It was very difficult to bathe myself or eat, or to have any normal bodily functions, because I was not identified with the body, but rather with universal, or cosmic, Self.

During my Samadhi states, my breathing stopped, my heart stopped beating, and I went into suspended animation for seven hours at a time, while the Divine Light and the Divine Voice entered into my body, and I merged into ecstatic bliss.

I became one with the universal or cosmic Self. It was totally unpredictable, and I never knew exactly on which day it would come. Initially, I had no control over it, but later on I learned how to go into the state voluntarily.

As Yogananda noted, it takes place now with less and less bodily fixation. The suspended animation is less, and I am now able to walk, open my eyes, talk on the phone and write down the experience while in it and pass it on to others through Darshan. The toll on the body gets less and less.

In past years, the days after the state "wore off" were always torturous. I used to experience a hangover type feeling, where the body felt burnt by the intensity of the Light. I would describe it as a 2000-volt charge of electricity going through a 50-watt bulb. The body would fry. Sometimes I felt my organs were going to burst, as the Light entered into me. At times, coming back into personality or individualized self again was unbearable. Occasionally, I couldn't get out of bed, or could hardly walk for three days after the experience.

And all along I went through all the experiences alone, unsupervised, and often with nobody to talk to who could understand. For years I could not tell anyone. There was always the fear that somebody would find my body while I was in Samadhi and thinking that it was dead, would dispose of it.

I have now been working on stabilizing the God communion- or deep absorption within the Self - into a permanent experience that can take place in the midst of daily worldly duties. Each time I have another Samadhi experience , I am made new. I am given a new body, a lighter body. All the old stuff drops away and I become sweet and smooth and renewed again. Each time I start all over again, with a new body, a new life.

When I am in Samadhi now, it appears that I can transfer it to others if they are open and receptive.

The key on the part of the receiver is innocence. If you're innocent, you're not analyzing, judging, doubting or being skeptical, and you can simply experience the moment. The experience itself is so simple. As soon as you bring mind into it, you lose it. As soon as you try to put it into a box, you've lost it.

You have to be free of concepts, open and innocent like a child, receptive and perceptive.

You cannot mood-make the experience. You can't think it into being or pretend that it's there. Mood making can be dangerous. Saying "I am God" if you are not experiencing it can be counter productive and dangerous for your ego.

The moment that you try to speak it or write it, you lose its essence because it is formless and conceptless. So it's made it very difficult to share this with humanity.

My prevailing feelings about my destiny are:

I've got to do, what cannot be done.

I've got to speak, what cannot be spoken.

I've got to teach, what cannot be taught.

I've got to do the impossible.

Be in the play, and act the part, while remaining awake,

knowing that I am not the play, nor the part.

I share this with you and trust that the reading of my direct experiences will impart some of the feeling of Samadhi into your being and awaken and activate your soul.

With Infinite Love,
Mirabai Devi

"See your heart blossoming into a beautiful
lotus flower and as you watch
the lotus petals unfolding
you see written on each petal
I deserve, I receive,
I am worthy, I am loved."
Mirabai Devi

"The highest reality is the Divine light. When you
surrender and let go, the Light comes
into you, because the Light is you."

Mirabai Devi

SAMADHI

Essence

of the

Divine

ON LIVING IN THE NOW

It's so simple.

When you hold onto stuff
it weighs you down
pulls you to live in the past.
When you let go, you're empty.

When you're empty
you're free to be in the now.
In the now you realize the Truth.

The truth is that it is so simple.

Realization happens in an instant.
So drop everything
all the baggage
all the stuff
and be in the now.

ON LOVE

The whole universe is made of love.

Every atom, every fiber, every cell:
it is all a creation of love,
created in love.

Very few experience this.

Those who do
experience who they truly are.

Fear separates and divides people.
Fear is created to keep people
separated from their soul
caught in the illusion of the
external world:
name-form-people-places-things,
so that few will know
that we are all part of God.

Some of us experience it
and know it consciously.

Fear keeps us stuck in ego
small self, personality.

That is what we identify with
thinking that that is who we are.

But identifying with who we are
on the outside
is our shell only.

Who we truly are within us is
infinite Spirit,
infinite Love.

We are Everything.

The entire universe
lives within us.

If you knew that everything is love,
you would never ever fear anything.

I feel and see the walls radiating
such peace, such bliss,
such intensive light
that it is dazzling to my eyes.

I experience everything as my Self.
You, me, the walls,
the background noises
everything in my
immediate environment
and everything in the whole
universe is my Self.

Everything is made of this
infinite Love.

What could we fear when we know or
experience this great Love?

When we know this Love
which is the highest level of reality,
then we can let go
of all
fear and separation
and become this Love.

My whole body is vibrating with this
warm, soft, brilliant Love.

My body
is part of everything else,
merged into everything
as omnipresent Love.

I rest in this Love
and am
totally at peace.

Everything, even the walls
are vibrating Love.

I know
that if everyone
could experience this infinite Love,
there would be
no pain
no suffering
no separation
no loneliness
and no fear.

This pulsating Love
that I am experiencing is
the Truth,
the highest level of reality.

All else is illusion.

I know
that whenever
I let go
I experience this Unity,
this infinite Love.

I know that it is an illusion
that we are separate.

It is our wrong identification
with the
false self
and
the outer reality
ego-form-separateness
that stops us
from experiencing Unity.

I am infinite love.

I am infinite peace.

I am infinite bliss.

I am infinite ecstasy.

I have always been
and
I will always be.

I am pure consciousness.

I am intoxicated with bliss,
free of human mind and ego.

Every moment is a new life,
a new opportunity.

The most important thing
is your Inner Self.

There is only the Inner Self.

Put your Inner Self first.

Take care of your Inner Self.

ON DIVINE LOVE

Divine Love is all consuming.

Divine Love is unconditional.

Divine Love
is without expectations
or attachment.

Divine Love
has nothing to do with
body and form,
but can express itself through
body and form.

Divine Love is what
causes us to incarnate and
play out this drama, or *leela*.

Divine Love is the reason for
the existence of life
and the cause of all creation.

Divine Love is
infinitely patient,
kind, and tolerant
like a mother with her child.

Divine Love is what holds
the stars,
galaxies,
and
universe together.

Divine Love
heals all
illness,
pain,
fear, problems
and
separation.

Divine Love is
the essence of who we are.

It is our nature,
our very essence.

To attain union
with our inner Divine Self
is the goal of Divine Love.

ON LONELINESS

A-lone-ness
is
all one ness.

All one-ness is who we are.

There is only one-the Self.

Loneliness is when
pain
is attached to
aloneness.

All one ness is when
joy
is experienced with
aloneness.

Tell
lonely people
to shift
their
wrong
identification

from the pain
of
small self

to the joy
of
big Self
from loneliness
to
all one ness!

Woman Seated in Deep Meditation

ON HOW YOU TREAT OTHERS

There is nobody else
but you.

You are everybody.

Therefore, how you treat anybody
is how you treat yourself.

Anything you do
to somebody else,
you are doing
to yourself.

ON LETTING GO

I am reminded again and again
of the one essential
and pure truth
that is at the essence
of all things,
and that is that
none of this is real.

We are all eternally
free and unbounded
and our ability to create
is beyond our perception.

We can truly relax and let go
and enjoy our lives,
which are beyond the drama of
pain and pleasure
and the limited filters of the ego.

All of this world
is illusion, maya.

We are the pulsating,
ecstatic, creative energy
of
Pure Life force
that is
beginningless and endless,
eternal and immortal.

If we can go beyond
the web of illusion
that sticks like glue
and know
the nature of our
own true Self,
which is everflowing
pure consciousness
that is setting us
eternally free,
then we can soar
like an eagle
into the greatest heights
never afraid of falling,
because there is
no up
and
no down.

ON REALIZATION OF SELF

Realization of Self.
It's so simple.
Everything else is complicated.

It's the very thing
we have always known.

It's that state that
underlies
everything.

We choose not to
be in
Permanent Self Realization
because we love
the drama so much,
because it's fun.

When we've had enough
of the drama
then we let go
and stay in
permanent Self Realization.

It's so simple
I just want to laugh and laugh.

There is
no me,
no you,
no people.

All forms are an equal expression
of the Divine Self,
the Universal Spirit
that is manifest in everything.

On the Highest Level of Consciousness

There is no good and no bad.

No right and no wrong.

All experiences are
just experiences.

Nothing on the outer
level of life matters.

I am the Omnipresent Self ,
manifest
in all things.

There is
only your Self,
only your Self,
only your Self.

Nowhere to go,
Nothing to do,
Only to be.

The reason you run away
from your Self
is only to lose yourself
in the drama.

But you will lose energy,
because no life
can be sustained
by the outer alone.

It must be charged
by the inner reality
of life itself.

There are many
different levels
to
every being,
but this is the
ultimate level of reality.

Remember
that there is
no separation,
only that
which is in
our minds.

All suffering
is what
we choose.

ON TRUTH

Remember
that what you have
always known
to be the Truth
is the Truth.

There is nothing to do.

Nowhere to go.

Nothing to achieve.

Nothing to attain.

We are everything.

Nothing matters.

Everybody
is
the Self.

No me and no you.

No struggle, no strain.

Nothing on the
outer level of life matters.

The whole of life
is
meaningless.

It has no meaning
and
no purpose,

except
for
the Self
to interact with
the Self
and experience
the Self.

All outer forms—illusion.

All outer activity—illusion.

All the business
of trying
to get somewhere: illusion.

There is nowhere to get to.

You are home now,

Be it.

Know it.

Experience it.

All moments
are equal and the same.
All places
are equal and the same.

We don't have to go anywhere.

We don't have to do anything.

We are everything
and everyone
and everywhere.

You don't have
to be concerned
whether anyone
likes you or not,
because they are you.

Grace happens
in the moment
when you let go
and
surrender to Love.

Mirabai in Her Light Body Self

ON TRANSFORMATION

Transform everything with love.

You are the Light.

Do not resist darkness,
If you resist—it sticks.
If you don't—it transforms.

Transform
the negativity
as it comes toward you
into Love.

Then all
that enters into you
is loved.
It becomes all Love.

Reaction is resistance
which causes negativity
to stick to you.

Thus
no resistance
and
no reaction—

Thus,
suffering is designed
to bring you
into bliss.

That is its nature!

What you resist
you become,
you experience.

If you resist
your Self,
you
will become
ignorant.

ON THE LAWS OF NATURE

Love.
Balance.
Neutrality.
Kindness.
Evolution.
Respect to all life forms.
Harmony.
Wholeness.

All these are the
laws of nature

Thus,
don't go out to
kill,
harm,
or
destroy.

Love is not an emotion.

It is a state of being.

ON DARKNESS

When in total darkness
or faced with darkness,
instead of resisting the darkness
Let the shift from
head to heart
take place.

Thus,
transform the darkness
by bringing
it into Love.

In other words,
experience the whole of life
from Beingness,
not from the head.

It is only in the face
of absolute darkness
that we can know
what absolute Light is.

That is why
we put ourselves
in the face
of our most opposite quality:
so that we can
see who we are.

We incarnate as
light into darkness
so that we can
experience and know
who we are.

Only in
absolute darkness
can you know the light.

Only when you experience
the deepest
and
the darkest pain
can you know
the most supreme joy.

There in the ugliest
most pain-ridden face
lies
the most precious
creator God.

Hiding
in the
ugliness
and
the blackness
is God
waiting to be found—
waiting to be revealed.

The most holy
is hiding
in the mud—
in the
darkest corner—

Waiting for eyes
that can see
to reveal Herself
so that She can set you free.

Liberate Her in every form.

Uncover every diamond
in the mud.

Every soul shines
through every body
if you reveal it.

Reveal God
in every
form.

ON ADVERSITY

Love the adversary.

Bring the adversary
into your
inner Self.

A state of Love.

But you have to attain
that state of Love first.

The adversary has lost the Self—

lost the Love,
that is the Self
in the illusion.

ON ENLIGHTENMENT

Enlightenment is the integration
of
absolute
and
relative realities.

Enlightenment
is when
the Self
is being
what it truly is.
Be who you are.
Naturalness of being.

Drop the disease of becoming
and
be who you are.

Working With the Light and the Light Beings

ON BEING IN ACTION

Nobody is special
because
everybody is special.

Keep the consciousness of
not doing anything.
Do everything wholeheartedly
but keep the consciousness
that you are not doing anything.

Because you simply are.
This is just the play.
Do not get lost in the game
that you are playing.
That is ego.

You are not the doer.

ON FORGIVENESS

Forgiveness
is
when you
realize that
you
are all
just
actors.

Everything is
yourself, so
no one or nothing
can hurt you or harm you
without you allowing it to be so.
So take responsibility
and forgive yourself for
your creation.

ON DESIRE

Desires from the small self
equal ignorance.

Ignorance is the loss of Self.
The One appears as many
for the play of consciousness
to take place.

Great desires
like for enlightenment,
world peace,
or to bring Heaven on earth
lead you to great expansion.

For what you focus on
you become.
To experience ourselves
is the original Desire.

ON SUFFERING

If we could take personal judgment
out of suffering
the suffering then becomes
a hammer or a screwdriver.

It's just a tool that can be used.
When you disown anything
as separate from the Self
then you are in resistance.

When you have resistance,
then you become separate
to the Self and become
the darkness of illusion.

Non resistance.
Non judgment.
Acceptance of
Is-ness.

When you are awake,
you can choose to learn
through joy instead of suffering.

ON HEALING

We don't love the disease.
We become Love.
We let the disease
enter into our Love.
Thereby it gets transformed.

By trying to
love or transform
with the
mind
or
emotions
we become the disease.

We empower the disease.
We have to remain
in a state of Love and
melt the disease
with the Divine Light.

Without reaction
or resistance
the disease is a catalyst
in order to bring us
into cosmic understanding
to learn our life lessons.

The only thing that
creates resistance
is
the small self
that doesn't feel loved.

Not loving the self.

All sickness
is due to a
lack of love.

Transmission of the Light in Light Body Self

71

ON FEAR

Fear
is the opposite of
love.
Fear is resistance.

Fear creates resistance
which creates pain.

Bring your fear
into your love.

Only through grace
can we do this.

God comes to us
in the form
of
our fears
as a teacher
to awaken us
from our illusions.

When we face
our imagined fears
we realize
that they are not real
and that only
God is real and true.

When we realize
that all we want
is the Light
then fear
is no longer needed
to awaken us.

In this sense, fear is love.

ON REMEMBERANCE

Remember
that a friend
in Truth
is a friend indeed.

Remember
you are not complete
until you are complete.

True wisdom
is
integrated experience.

ON NOTHING AND EVERYTHING

Nothing
on the outer level of life matters.
It is all an illusion.

The only thing
that is real
is the inner Self
that pervades everything.
My Self is in all forms
and experiences this.

I don't even need
to open my eyes
and look at the outer,
because of the appearance of separation.
Many names and forms
that create separation
and are not real.

There is nothing to do
to strive for
to attain or to get.

There is no lack or limitation.
I have everything
because I am everything.
All is contained in me.
Therefore, all I have to do
is to relax in the bliss
to experience the bliss
which is my nature
which is the Self.

There is no need to strain
no effort required
just to be in this perpetual
state of peace and eternal bliss
enjoying my true Being
because that is all there is.

Everything is made and composed
of this indescribable peace.

ON DUALITY

On the ultimate level of life,
there is no judgement of good or bad,
or of right and wrong.

Only the judgments of our own mind.

There is no here and no there.

We live in a world of energy and light.

We stage this grand play
of physical form to know
and experience ourselves.

Without judgment
criticism
and
self-condemnation
we are
free to be.

HOW CAN WE EXPERIENCE UNITY CONSCIOUSNESS

You cannot obtain Samadhi
until you are ready.

It is an experience
that comes naturally by itself.

However
there are things you can do
to prepare yourself for it.

All the enlightened masters
prescribe doing
selfless service
meditation
mantra
cleansing
prayers
forgiveness
and yoga
to purify the mind
by focusing
on the Divine.

"God feels compassion for your pain and wants to
take your pain. Your pain does not belong with you;
it belongs with God. It has to be offered back and
surrendered up. All that then remains is your
Divine nature, which is pure love,
compassion and kindness."

Mirabai Devi

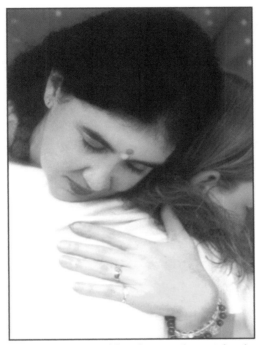

"The more you are able to let go and surrender, the
more the Divine can work in your life. Either you
let go, or you hold on and suffer."

Mirabai Devi

Mirabai Devi Foundation

The mission of **Mirabai Devi** and the **Mirabai Devi Foundation** is to help humanity return home to God and the Light, raise the consciousness of the planet, and so bring liberation and world peace. Mirabai's work includes Darshan, the transmission of the Divine Light, healing work, sacred service and spiritual practice.

Darshan – Transmission of the Divine Light

The **Mirabai Devi Foundation** is devoted to making Darshan available to as many people as possible. Darshan is open to people from all faiths and paths, so that all people can experience their direct connection to the transforming universal Light, which transcends all religions and is the essence of all.

Darshan creates a sacred space where people can come in community to be awakened, healed, and nurtured. During Darshan, people can release their pain and impurities, and the Light will open them up to transmute their negative karma and trauma, fill them with Shakti (Divine Feminine Power) and activate their inner Light. The transmission of Light that occurs during Darshan with Mirabai Devi is not dependent on time or space for anyone to receive it.

It is not the purpose of Darshan to replace a person's personal, religious practice. It is meant to support a deeper trust and faith in the Divine Light. Coming to Darshan does not bind you in any way to Mirabai Devi or to the Mirabai Devi Foundation. It is a gift, freely given to be shared and made accessible to all, regardless of one's belief system.

Healing

Healing occurs through reaching the cause of the problem, pain or illness.Through the spiritual art of peacemaking, forgiveness, prayer and transmission of the Divine Light, burdens, pain and problems can be transmuted and released. This allows you to return back to your natural state.

Spiritual Practice

Once the transmission of the Divine Light is received it is integrated into our lives through daily spiritual practice. These practices include mantra, chanting, forgiveness prayers, meditation, breath work and yoga, or spiritual exercise.

Sacred Service

Through service we transmute our negative karma and earn Divine Grace. When we serve others, we bring the expression of their divinity to the surface and allow them to shine.

The Foundation's Sacred Service includes the creation of events, retreats, workshops, meditation groups, Lightworker trainings and world peace prayer days.

The Mirabai Devi Foundation supports AIDS orphanages and meditation colleges in South Africa, and sponsors and supports spiritual teachers and healers in their work. It distributes spiritual teachings through books, CDs and DVDs, teleconferences and webinars.

The Mirabai Devi Foundation supports a new paradigm of spiritual teaching. This paradigm integrates the Light into physical form, embodies abundance, leads us to face our pain and overcome our challenges. It empowers us to be fully ourselves.

If you would like to receive more information about Mirabai Devi's work,
contact us at
info@mirabaidevi.org

Or visit the Foundation's website at
www.mirabaidevi.org

For further teachings on mantras,
contact Thomas Ashley Farrand at
www.sanskritmantra.com

To download copies of the forgiveness prayers,
contact Howard Wills at
www.howardwills.com

.

CPSIA information can be obtained
at www.ICGtesting.com
Printed in the USA
LVIW011433171212
312064LV00001B